My friends have he  sat with me in the playoff game, brough~~t me food when I was sick~~, put up with my weird ideas of fun when I'm well, and been available 24/7 when things were both horrible and amazing.

Some of these friends I am talking about are still in my life, and texting me silly things as I sit here writing.

Others no longer are, for a multitude of reasons. Writing about them pulls up a similar sense of grief in me as writing about my late husband.

Extraordinary loss does that to a person.

You Know What Sucks? Really Fucking Bad? Friendship Breakups.

I am always touching base with friends, family, colleagues, and my online posse when I am writing on a new subject. I swear, I have never had such an immediate, hard-core reaction on a topic than when I asked for feedback on the topic of friendship breakups. In my therapy consultation group, everyone admitted that they had an immediate flashback to that one broken friendship experience the minute I asked. Why does this topic trigger EVERYONE?

I think it comes from the cultural expectations and norms we have about friendship. When you think about it, we have far more realistic expectations about romantic relationships than we do friendships. And we have a way better handle on dealing with the fall-out when they fail.

As a general rule, relationships DON'T last until death do us part...but there is way more pressure on our friendships than there is on our relationships. And when they don't last, we have no fucking clue how to deal. So what's the malfunction?

Letty Pogrebin, in her book *Among Friends* (1987) notes that there are four epic contradictions in how we experience our friendships. I had never read read anything that summed up the issue so well , and it made sense to me. And I think we really could conceptualize why friendships fail by understanding makes them so stressful to begin with.

1) **The Stress Factor.** In ye olden days of yore, friendships were stress relievers. No pressure, the fun part of our lives. But now they are stress producers, something else we have to manage along with all the other shit in our lives.

2) **Lack of Consensus.** We all use the word friendship but all have totally different ideas of what friendship means. Different *meanings* equal different *expectations* equals *epic fails.*

3) **The Critical Stance.** We expect more from friends than from family. This seems backwards, but it make sense. Family is chosen for us, friends are something we choose. But you know how we choose our friends? Based on the sense of loyalty and trust we feel from them. More than shared social status or any other friendship determination factor, we are attracted to people with *value systems* similar to our own. They reinforce and validate our beliefs about the world, and they make us feel safest in our interactions with them and with others. They have our backs, so to speak. So we expect way more expert awesomeness from them, and get way more butthurt when they are human and fail to meet our expectations. Makes sense, right? You can't un-family Uncle Cyril for being a racist creeper, but you can definitely un-friend someone whose values don't align with your own.

4) Self-Reliance Vs. Connection. Pogrebin's book predates the neuro research that shows we are hardwired to connect to others, but she nailed it when she said we have a deep seated desire for intimate connection with others but a cultural message that we should be self-reliant and protect our privacy. What's the first to go if we feel overwhelmed? Not our family whom we have blood connections to. Not our mates, whom we have legal connections to. Our friends are the ones that we dump out first. But then the world tells us be self-reliant. And we start feeling weirded out and guilty for all this stuff our bestie now knows. So we get all fucking weird around them and are trying to pull back. But it doesn't really work like that, does it?

All of these things equate to serious pressure in the end. Friendships end up carrying more weight than many of them can really end up bearing for a sustained amount of time. Because friendship is hard work. And people change. And circumstances change. And the very mechanisms that create friendships are often what lead to their dissolution.

Is it Over? Like, Really For Reals Over?

Maybe you are reading this because your friendship is the over-ist over that ever over'd. But maybe not. Maybe you aren't sure what to do in this situation. Are you kinda going back and forth on this friendship break up thing? Let's discuss.

First of all: Is it something they **DID** or something they **ARE**? You know what I mean here. Are they so fundamentally in a place that is dangerous for you in some way shape or form? Or did they just fuck up?

And when I say "just" I don't mean that it wasn't a big deal. Fuck ups can be huge, nasty messes. But is it indicative of how they generally navigate the world and treat others? Or is it a genuine mistake or lapse of judgment? Is this an issue that has the potential to be corrected if it is discussed and new boundaries are established? If you were the one who fucked up, how would you hope people would approach you?

A lot of times we allow certain behaviors long enough that they become the norm. When we allow people to do certain things or treat us in a certain way, they are more than likely going to continue to do so until we stop them. If your friend is generally a good and excellent person and may respond to you setting new boundaries, it's worth trying to have that conversation before you go into break-up mode.

Or it may be that you can tolerate the behavior at a different level. For example, if you have the perpetually late/no-show friend who you otherwise dig, maybe only invite them to hang out when it's a group gathering where their arrival time won't impact festivities. Let them be their late-ass self on those occasions, but have the expectation is different ("Movie starts at 6:30, not 7:15 and I'm not waiting for your ass! So if you can't be on time tell me now and I'll make different plans!").

Are you willing to make the first move on this?

Cuz we all fuck up. And sometimes owning our shit and apologizing is the most difficult thing ever. And we've all been there. Sometimes people will fade out rather than owning their shit and apologizing. Are you willing to start the conversation?

"Hey, I want to talk about what happened. I was really pissed off and confused when you didn't show up last week and then we haven't talked since. I'd like to talk about it if you are willing."

Guess what? Adulting time. That doesn't let your friend off the hook for what they did, but you do need to take responsibility for your part when you have the conversation.

What is Friend-Person's responsibility here?

What was the specific behavior that upset you? What was your response to that behavior? You want to frame it just like that. "When you_, I felt_."

What is your responsibility here?

Is there anything that you did in this situation that you need to take responsibility for? Did you not establish or enforce your boundaries? Did you respond to your friend in a way that you are ashamed of or embarrassed about? Did you do or say anything that made the situation worse? Like…if there was a video playback of your behavior in this situation, are there any parts of the tape that would make you cringe?

"I realize you I told you it was OK, when I really wasn't OK."

"I realize that I screamed at you when you didn't show up, which was a shitty way of communicating my feelings."

What do you want to happen differently in the future for the friendship to maintain?

And this is the other part of communicating effectively. After explaining what bothered you and how it made you feel, you want to ask for the behavior you want instead. "What I am asking for is_."

What will their role be in what you want instead?

You have requested a different behavior, now explain exactly what change this entails on their part.

"I am asking you to_."

What will you yours be?

And explain your understanding of what your role will be.

"I know that I have responsibility here, too, and I want to make this better. I will do_."

Ok, so you tried the thing. Maybe eleventy times. Or maybe it was way not salvageable, and that's OK too. This is the part where you put on your grown-person pants and come up with a proper break-up plan. Because you are not Berger and post-it break-ups are still the dickest move ever.

If You Are The Breaker-Upper

Leslie Baxter's 1982 study (cited in Pogrebin's book) studied all the different ways that people end friendships and came up with four main categories"

- Withdrawal and Avoidance — Basic ghosting. Just pulling away, avoiding contact, trying to let it die off on its own.

- Intentional Manipulation — Creating a hostile friend environment so the friend gets tired of your shit and dumps you.

- Strategies of Positive Concern — This is the *"it's not you, it's me"* convo. I'm not in a good place, I'm not good for you right now, etc., etc.

- Open Confrontation — Whether calm or explosive, calling out the ending for what it is.

So, of these types there are really only two that won't register on the Berger scale if done right. Let's look at these options.

Ghosting

Let's be honest, this is what happens more often or not. Since we don't have any real mechanism for friendship break ups, we usually end up just ghosting them out.

This isn't always a dick move, actually. If it's a mutual agreement type situation, where you both just fade away from each other, no foul, it can be the best mechanism for dealing with the issue, especially if you have a shared social circle. You cool, it's not a THING, but…you just grew apart and aren't really just hanging out together anymore. It's cool if you both end up at the same party, you know? Not a problem. Just…you know how things go.

A really interesting conference paper on Facebook defriending (Sibona and Walczak, 2011) noted that while friending is an active request and accept process, defriending isn't. They didn't study this particular part of the equation, but it did make me wonder if that makes the idea of ghosting out a friend feel easier and more acceptable at some level because social media has created a mechanism for doing so, at least for online relationships.

Oh, and if you misjudge this relationship as a fade-away and get called out for ghosting? Own that shit and apologize.

#ByeFelicia

Sometimes? Sometimes just no. Sometimes you just can't even work this shit out, and they are not in agreement in the mutual fade-away.

Sometimes they end up in such a diametrically opposite place than you are that having them in your life isn't going to be healthy for either one of you.

But the slow fade isn't working. And manipulating them into breaking up with you, or pulling some "it's not you, it's me" bullshit is way too dick a move, for serious.

You have to be grown and have the convo. Pull up your grown person pants and do the things:

1) **Tell them the reason.** You don't have to be all bashing of their dickitude. But tell the truth, owning your response to their behavior. Remember, no one MAKES you feel a certain way. "Hey, Friend-Person? You have been partying hard lately, at least by

my standards. You seem really happy and having fun, but it's not been something I'm comfortable with. I'm focusing on my job right now, and partying isn't good for me. I think at this point our lives are going in different directions, and maintaining a friendship isn't possible for me. I wish all the best for you."

2) **Discuss the semantics.** What are they? You don't want to see them ever again? You are fine to hang out at group events but don't wanna do bestie stuff anymore? What does this break up actually entail? "I know I'll see you at Steve's party in a couple weeks and I'm totally cool with that if you are, but hanging out one on one isn't something I want to do anymore."

3) **Tell other concerned parties.** But FFS, don't ask them to take sides. Tell them the facts and what your break-up entiails. If you hear rumor mill about your Ex-BFF trashing you, ask your peeps to cease spreading the word. "Not being friends with Ex-BFF has been hard enough, I don't want to make things worse by shit talking them or hearing any gossip, but thanks for being worried about us."

4) Figure out how you want to deal with the social media aspect. I suggest the minimum necessary separation. It's already a big enough thing happening, right? Defriending them makes life easier? Let them know that is what's gonna happen. But don't do the whole blocking thing, unless they are dropping bombs all over your accounts and you really fucking have to. And unless they have gone batshit and you are in active blocking mode, let them know what's going on.

If You Are The Breaker-Upee

My son is in high school. When we were discussing the epic douchery behind shitty friendship breakups, I realized that what he is dealing with is no less mature than what I see adults dealing with on a daily basis (and have dealt with myself).

It just feeds into my best friend's theory that the human race is operationally still all in high school and if we could just get ourselves up to undergrad status we might actually be able to affect some real change.

I also asked my son how he dealt with friendship breakups. He said, in the way only a monosyllabic teenage linebacker can:

"I dunno, it like, takes a while. There's, like, stages... or something."

You mean like Elizabeth Kubler-Ross's stages of grief?

"Huh?"

Ugh, yeah. Nevermind, bro. But he's right. And he's kinda a savant, isn't he? He's never heard of Kubler-Ross but nailed it on the head when he said that all endings have a process attached to them. We don't necessarily honor that in regards to friendship, but we SHOULD. So let's talk about how the Stages of Grief apply to friendship break-ups.

Denial – What? Nothing's wrong. Their just busy and whatever. We are as close as we always have been. Ok, I can see they read my text and didn't respond. But they will later, I'm sure. LALALALA, we are FINE.

Anger – Stupid ass. I'm awesome and they are a SHITHEAD. I'm going to tell them this. I'm going to tell everyone else this. I'm mad because (1) I'm hurt and (2) My expectations about this person weren't met. (And have you read my anger zine? You totally should!) I feel raw and reactionary and all kinds of awful things.

Bargaining – This is the desperate and hurt part of us peeking out from behind the anger response. Trying to figure out how to hostage negotiate this system back into safety. Sometimes bargaining works to a certain extent. You cave in on YOUR values and relationship expectations in order to try to maintain a dying relationship. And end up feeling worse in the long run. Other times no matter what you do they are just GONE, and you feel like a pushover for trying to bargain them back. Bargaining is a really normal impulse, though. It's our brain trying to create some homeostasis by snagging back what it feels is missing and necessary.

Depression — This is where the reality part kicks in. This person was your friend and you got dumped. And it hurts like hell. But there are no sad breakup movies for friendship. And Ben and Jerry's hasn't yet developed a flavor honoring our need to get fucked up on ice cream in our PJs because our bestie dumped us. Avoidance of this part of the process is where we cause ourselves the most harm, I've found. Own what you are feeling. Trying to quash it will make it fester, breathing through it is how we best move on.

Acceptance — This is the part where the breathing doesn't have to take such a *fucking conscious effort*. It's not necessarily all better, but it's livable again. You are at a place where you know that it's done and you are letting go.

But I Misses Them!!

Of course you do, love.

Here is the other thing to remember. The stages of grief things is NOT a linear, step-wise process. It's recursive, and full of relapses. And remorse. And regret. And remembering.

Lots of RE words. *Re* is a Latin prefix that means "again and again." It's indicative of that cyclical way emotions and memories work. The acceptance stage isn't a magical place of all betterness and calorie-free Nacho Cheese Doritos.

And that's OK. Nobody heals from a loss in a complete and logical way because human beings aren't wired to be like that. It's OK to think you are over Ex-Friend and then find yourself with a urge to Facebook stalk them to see who their new bestie is. Or to try to reconnect and work things out.

Best thing to do? Take a deep breath. Acknowledge the serious missing going on and what you are feeling. But think about the following:

1) What is the best thing that can happen here? You realize that no one else

loves them the same and they are miserable and will change their evil ways and be an excellent friend again?

2) **What is the worst thing that can happen?** You will see they don't give AF that you are not in their life anymore? That they will totally get back together with you and then treat you like shit all over again?

3) What's the **MOST LIKELY** thing that will happen? And you know the answer to this, you totally do. Will trying to dig back into this relationship end in an emotional ass kicking for you? You know, *most likely?*

You are grown, and you can do whatever you want, of course.

But seriously, honey?

Don't do the thing. It's akin to putting your hand on a stove that you know is likely going to be hot. You know the getting burned thing is gonna happen, don't you? Think of it as you would a romantic relationship that ended for the betterment of your (emotional, physical, and mental) health. Think of what you would tell someone you loved beyond all measure about to do something that was going to end up with them being hurt. You would do everything in your power to protect them, right? Because they are worthy of care and protection. And you are, too. Take care of your precious self the way you would anyone else you adore. And don't let a toxic friendship kick your ass again after you already escaped it.

Moving On and Finding Ways To Be OK

The moving on part is tough. Like all other forms of grief, this shit TAKES TIME. And you get to give yourself that time. And it's OK to reach out to other friends for support.

Remember a few pages back when we talked about the cultural expectations about friendships never ending and the lack of cultural ritual we have for letting them go?

The good part of that is that you get to create whatever grieving ritual or process you need in order to make your healing happen.

What do you need right now?

As I was writing this section, I got an email from a friend—we're gonna call him Bob—who had been struggling with a particularly nasty friendship breakup, where he was being excluded from a large social circle of which he had been a member for some time. It was a situation where he was taken completely by surprise and felt ganged-up-upon. He didn't know this was one of my current writing projects, but gave me permission to share his email when I explained that he just participated in one of those universe-confluence moments by touching upon exactly what I was struggling to articulate.

Many, many thanks to Bob.

This weekend was our church's men's retreat. Friday night opened with an ice breaker where the leader asked us to share what light we bring into the world and what keeps if from shining. People got seriously deep seriously fast. I think it was the second guy that got to *"I've never spoken this [shame] aloud to anyone."* I was near the last. My light is that *"I'm freaking awesome and I'm not afraid to do things other people are"* or if you ask my friends it is that I really actually listen. The second bit was shared with the context of the recent friend break up and how I had asked people for affirmations to counteract the negative messages I was receiving. After I was done, someone spoke up to the group and said, *"I always thought the idea of a best friend was kind of stupid and something for middle school girls. But, over the last few weeks I've realized Bob is the best friend I've ever had."* That certainly caught me off guard.

The theme of the retreat was how we find the light shining in the darkness. There was a lot of focus on the darkness part, and as I was sitting and listening I kept thinking, *"this isn't were I am right now."* Despite all the blunders I've had in the last two months I've had lots of affirmation from friends and my wife that have me feeling great.

Bob had actively sought the support and affirmation he needed in the process of losing not just one friend, but an entire group of friends and acquaintances. When he sat back and reflected on the process, he realized that he felt way better about the situation than he had realized because he had been self-aware and proactive in his own healing process.

It's OK to be hurting, it's OK to grieve, and it's OK to ask for help. If you were in a terrible car accident, no one would tell you to toughen up. They'd bring you to the hospital immediately. Everyone needs care at critical times, but not everyone realizes what times are critical.

It's OK to identify what you need, articulate
that need, and seek it out from others and from
within yourself. That is what light shining
through the darkness is all about.

FaithGHarper.com

$4 U.S. / $4.99 CANADA

ISBN 978-1-62106-034-5   US$4.00

50400>

9 781621 060345